EVERYTHING SPORTS ALMANACS

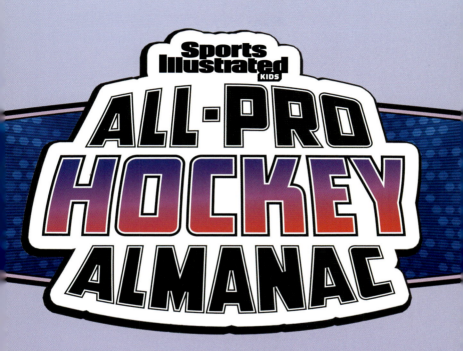

BY ELLIOTT SMITH

CAPSTONE PRESS
a capstone imprint

Published by Capstone Press, an imprint of Capstone
1710 Roe Crest Drive, North Mankato, Minnesota 56003
capstonepub.com

Copyright © 2026 by Capstone. All rights reserved. No part of this publication may be reproduced in whole or in part, or stored in a retrieval system, or transmitted in any form or by any means, electronic, mechanical, photocopying, recording, or otherwise, without written permission of the publisher.

SPORTS ILLUSTRATED KIDS is a trademark of ABG-SI LLC. Used with permission.

Library of Congress Cataloging-in-Publication Data is available on the Library of Congress website.

ISBN: 9798875232824 (hardcover)
ISBN: 9798875232770 (paperback)
ISBN: 9798875232787 (ebook PDF)

Summary: Exciting pro hockey facts in a variety of formats keep excited sports fans turning the page.

Quote Sources:
p. 23, "Connor Bedard and Trevor Zegras Score Lacrosse-style Goals on NHL's Final Night Before Break," published December 24, 2023, foxsports.com/articles/nhl/connor-bedard-and-trevor-zegras-score-lacrossestyle-goals-on-nhls-final-night-before-break, Accessed February 12, 2025
p. 39, "Willie O'Ree 'Overwhelmed and Thrilled' as His Jersey No. 22 Is Finally Retired by Boston Bruins," by Greg Wyshynski, published January 18, 2022,, foxsports.com/articles/nhl/connor-bedard-and-trevor-zegras-score-lacrossestyle-goals-on-nhls-final-night-before-break, Accessed February 12, 2025

Editorial Credits
Editor: Mandy Robbins; Designer: Sarah Bennett; Media Researcher: Rebekah Hubstenberger; Production Specialist: Tori Abraham

Image Credits
Associated Press: Jae C. Hong, 22 (top), Ray Lussier/The Boston Herald, 21 (bottom), The Canadian Press/Sean Kilpatrick, 25 (middle); Getty Images: A-Digit, 23 (goalie silhouette), alikemalkarasu, 14, Bruce Bennett, front cover (top), 13, Carmen Mandato, 31 (top), Christian Petersen,10, Connect Images (puck), back cover, 23, Dave Sandford, 18, David Berding, 19 (bottom right), Derek Cain, 37, Derek Leung, 44 (bottom), Eliot J. Schechter/NHLI, 16, Elsa, 15, Ethan Miller, 11, 36 (bottom), 46 (middle), Frederick Breedon, 47 (middle), Harry How, 40, iStock/Chorna Olena, 41 (rink), iStock/envastudio (dots), throughout, Jamie Sabau, 19 (top), Jared Silber/NHLI, 45, Jason Mowry, 24 (top), Joel Auerbach, 4, 12, Jonathan Daniel, 26-27 (top), Mark Blinch/NHLI, 17, Mike Carlson, 31 (bottom left), Minas Panagiotakis, 5 (top), miniature, 6 (map), Patrick Smith, front cover (bottom left), Rakdee (hockey icons), 36, 41, 44, Rich Gagnon, 39 (middle), Rick Stewart, 35, Scott Halleran/Allsport, 42 (middle), Scott Olson, 33, Sean M. Haffey, front cover (bottom right), Steph Chambers, 8, Troy Parla, 43 (bottom), XonkArts, 25 (top right); Shutterstock: A.j.K, 27 (top right), alanto, 46 (top and bottom), 47 (bottom), Arrobani Studio, 10-11 (gold background), Begimail, 5 (bottom left), Darryl Brooks, 7 (top), Fallen Knight (holographic background), cover and throughout, halwani wani, 42-43 (net background overlay), Here, 38-39 (background), Igillustrator, 47 (bottom left), Ilya Lukichev, 21 (top), mentalmind (stars and ribbon), 8, 36, 44, Oleksii Sidorov, 32, Olga Moonlight, 3 (background), siart (ice rink background), throughout, StarLine, back cover (background), tomambroz (Stanley cup icon), 30, 34, tovovan, 7 (bottom), Vectorpocket, 6 (background), Yehor Zinchenko, 23 (hockey players silhouette); Sports Illustrated: John Iacono, 29, Manny Millan, 28

Any additional websites and resources referenced in this book are not maintained, authorized, or sponsored by Capstone. All product and company names are trademarks™ or registered® trademarks of their respective holders.

* * * All stats are current through April 8, 2025. * * *

```
Printed and bound in the USA.   006307
```

Table of Contents

About the League 4

Greatest Games 12

Standout Plays 20

Team Dynasties 28

Iconic Players 34

Record Breakers 42

About the League

History and Growth

The National Hockey League (NHL) began in 1917 with four Canadian teams. In the following years, American teams joined while Canadian teams folded. For nearly 25 years, the NHL had just six teams—the Boston Bruins, Chicago Blackhawks, Detroit Red Wings, Montreal Canadiens, New York Rangers, and Toronto Maple Leafs.

From 1967 to 2021, the league added 26 teams! The NHL drew a record 22.9 million fans in the 2023–24 season.

NOT JUST A NORTHERN SPORT
Hockey is even popular in warm-weather places. Star Auston Matthews grew up playing the game in Arizona.

1	Boston Bruins
2	Chicago Blackhawks
3	Detroit Red Wings
4	Montreal Canadiens
5	New York Rangers
6	Toronto Maple Leafs

The Original SIX

These six teams are known as the NHL's Original Six. They made up the entirety of the league from 1942 to 1967.

BLOW THAT HORN!

Fans love the horn noise made when their team scores a goal. But the horn wasn't introduced until 1973. The Chicago Blackhawks were the first team to use one. The team's owner liked the sound of the horn on his yacht. So, he installed it at the stadium.

HOW POINTS ARE SCORED

The NHL uses a point system for both players and teams when it comes to records and standings.

FOR PLAYERS

2 points for each goal
+
1 point for each assist
―――――――――――――
= TOTAL POINTS

FOR TEAMS

2 points for each win
+
1 point for each overtime loss
―――――――――――――
= TOTAL POINTS

STARS OF THE GAME

At the end of each NHL game, three players are awarded stars for their good play. This tradition started in 1936. Now, members of the local media award the three stars every night. The winning players take the ice for a final skate.

» Brandon Montour of the Seattle Kraken holds a stuffed toy salmon after being named a Star of the Game against the Nashville Predators in 2024.

NHL TEAMS AND THEIR DIVISIONS

EASTERN CONFERENCE

Atlantic Division	Metropolitan Division
Boston Bruins	Carolina Hurricanes
Buffalo Sabres	Columbus Blue Jackets
Detroit Red Wings	Philadelphia Flyers
Florida Panthers	Pittsburgh Penguins
Montreal Canadiens	New Jersey Devils
Ottawa Senators	New York Islanders
Tampa Bay Lightning	New York Rangers
Toronto Maple Leafs	Washington Capitals

WESTERN CONFERENCE

Central Division	Pacific Division
Chicago Blackhawks	Anaheim Ducks
Colorado Avalanche	Calgary Flames
Dallas Stars	Edmonton Oilers
Minnesota Wild	Los Angeles Kings
Nashville Predators	San Jose Sharks
St. Louis Blues	Vancouver Canucks
Winnipeg Jets	Vegas Golden Knights
Utah Hockey Club*	Seattle Kraken

The Utah Hockey Club is the unofficial name of the NHL's newest expansion team. A 2025 naming contest let the fans choose the official name.

A GOLDEN SUCCESS STORY

The Vegas Golden Knights joined the NHL in 2017. Their players were pulled from every other team in the league.

The first-year team qualified for the Stanley Cup Final. While the Knights fell short against the Washington Capitals, it was a great beginning for the team.

The Knights returned to the Stanley Cup Final in 2023. This time, The Knights beat the Florida Panthers to win the Cup.

PUTTING ON A SHOW

The Knights changed the pregame experience for fans. Before each game, there is an elaborate show. The team's mascot battles someone who represents their opponent in a showdown filled with lights, fire, and fantastic special effects.

Greatest Games

GAME 7

The **2024 Stanley Cup Final** between the **Edmonton Oilers** and the **Florida Panthers** came down to Game 7.

The **Oilers** had come back from being down three games to none to being tied at three games apiece.

The **Panthers** were looking to win the first Cup in franchise history after losing in the championship the year before.

Florida took an early 1-0 lead.

Edmonton tied it a few minutes later.

The **Panthers' Sam Reinhart** scored the game-winning goal in the second period. His teammates held off the Oilers and won the Cup!

»Reinhart scores the game-winning goal.

LONGEST GAME IN NHL HISTORY

In the regular season, games can end in a tie. But in the playoffs, games continue until a winner is decided. That has made for some long games over the years.

LONG GAME
Anaheim Mighty Ducks vs. Dallas Stars (2003)
5 overtimes, 140 minutes, 48 seconds

Columbus Blue Jackets vs. Tampa Bay Lightning (2020)
5 overtimes, 150 minutes, 27 seconds

Philadelphia Flyers vs. Pittsburgh Penguins (2000)
5 overtimes, 152 minutes, 1 second

Boston Bruins vs. Toronto Maple Leafs (1933)
6 overtimes, 164 minutes, 46 seconds

LONGEST GAME!
Detroit Red Wings vs. Montreal Maroons (1936)
6 overtimes, 176 minutes, 30 seconds

» Pierre-Luc Dubois of the Blue Jackets smacks the puck as Mitchell Stephens and Andrei Vasilevskiy defend the net during the second of five overtime periods in 2020.

HIGHEST-SCORING GAME

The highest-scoring game in NHL history happened on December 11, 1985. The Edmonton Oilers beat the Chicago Blackhawks 12–9. Oilers Hall of Famer Wayne Gretzky finished the night with seven assists.

LONGEST SHOOT-OUT!

The longest shoot-out in NHL history happened on December 16, 2014. The Florida Panthers and Washington Capitals went 20 shoot-out rounds before the Panthers finally won. The game had the most shoot-out goals at 11 and the most shoot-out saves with 15.

» Nick Bjugstad shoots and scores against goaltender Braden Holtby in the longest shoot-out in NHL history.

»David Ayres makes a save as emergency goalie.

Emergency In Net

In February 2020, the Carolina Hurricanes were in trouble. Both their goalies were injured in their game against the Toronto Maple Leafs. The Hurricanes had to use the NHL's emergency goalie system. This is a person at the stadium that either team can use in an injury situation. The emergency goalie was 42-year-old David Ayres. He was a Zamboni driver and maintenance worker for the Maple Leafs' minor league team.

Ayres had never played in the NHL. He quickly gave up two goals before settling in. Ayers made saves on the final eight shots. The Hurricanes won 6–3. Ayres was named the star of the game. He was paid $500 and allowed to keep his game-worn jersey.

THE *COOLEST* WINTER CLASSICS

The NHL Winter Classic is a series of outdoor games that take hockey back to its roots. It's often held on New Year's Eve or New Year's Day.

THE FIRST

» The first Winter Classic was held January 1, 2008, in Orchard Park, New York, between the Sabres and Penguins.

RECORD CROWD

» In 2014, the Winter Classic was held at Michigan Stadium. More than 105,000 fans came out to see the Maple Leafs beat the Red Wings.

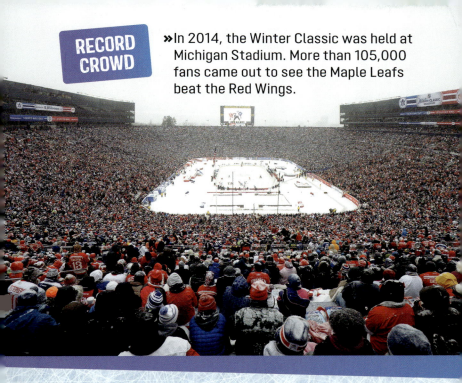

THE COLDEST

» The 2022 game at Target Field in Minneapolis was the coldest in the series. The temperature at the start was -6 degrees Fahrenheit (-14 degrees Celsius). Players from both the Wild and the Blues had icicles form in their beards!

Ryan O'Reilly

Standout Plays

BOBBY ORR'S HIGH-FLYING SHOT

Bobby Orr is an NHL legend. The defenseman made one of the greatest goals in history.

In the 1970 Stanley Cup Finals, Orr's Boston Bruins were up 3–0 over the St. Louis Blues. Game 4 went to overtime. Orr passed to teammate Derek Sanderson behind the net. Orr then skated toward the center of the ice. Sanderson gave him a quick pass, and Orr fired the puck between the goalie's legs for the winning goal.

As he started to celebrate, Orr's skates were clipped by a Blues defender. Orr went soaring through the air like Superman. The stunning image was captured by a photographer.

»The photo of Bobby Orr soaring through the air is one of the most memorable scenes in hockey history.

»Trevor Zegras scores "a Michigan" against the Kraken in 2023.

TREVOR ZEGRAS
THE MICHIGAN

The Anaheim Ducks' Trevor Zegras has a special skill when it comes to scoring goals. He's used a unique stick move to tally at least three lacrosse-style goals in games. Zegras cradles the puck on his stick and flings it into the net the way a lacrosse player does. This type of goal is called "a Michigan." It was named after University of Michigan player Mike Legg, who scored such a goal in a 1996 game.

HOW'D HE SCORE THAT GOAL?

THE WRAPAROUND

THE SCOOP — From behind the net, Zegras scoops up the puck and balances it on the flat front of his stick, like a lacrosse player.

THE FLING! — In one swift move, Zegras wraps around the side of the net and flings the puck past the goalie to score.

"In my opinion, it's not like a crazy play for me to do," Zegras says of his amazing goals.

Alex Nedeljkovic

GOALIE GREATNESS

On January 17, 2025, Pittsburgh Penguins goaltender Alex Nedeljkovic became the first goalie to have both an assist and a goal in the same game. The Penguins beat the Sabres 5–2.

SLAP SHOT SPEED

The fastest slap shot in NHL history is 108.8 miles (175 kilometers) per hour. Former Boston Bruin Zdeno Chára achieved this feat during the 2012 NHL All-Star game.

»Zdeno Chára wins the hardest shot event with his record-setting shot at the 2012 NHL All-Star skills hockey competition.

HATS OFF TO YOU

Scoring three goals in a game is no easy feat. It's called a hat trick. There were 115 hat tricks in the 2023–24 NHL season.

In the 1940s, a Montreal hat store offered a free hat to any player who scored three goals in a game at the Montreal Forum. The hat trick grew in popularity from there.

At NHL arenas, fans celebrate hat tricks by throwing their hats onto the ice. During big games, hundreds of hats can litter the ice.

HIGH 5

These active players have made five goals in one NHL game.

Tage Thompson
December 7, 2022

Timo Meier
January 17, 2022

Mika Zibanejad
March 5, 2020

Patrik Laine
November 24, 2018

Some teams display the hats in the arena. Others donate them to local charities. A few offer the hats to the player in honor of his big day. Some teams even let fans get their hats back!

Joe Malone set the NHL record for most goals in a game back in 1920 with seven.

Team Dynasties

Striking Oil

Starting in 1984, Wayne Gretzky led the Oilers to five championships in seven seasons. Gretzky was the team's star, but the Oilers were not a one-man show. Players like Mark Messier and Grant Fuhr were key to the championship run. Seven dynasty players and coach Glen Sather made it into the Hockey Hall of Fame.

Even after Gretzky was traded to Los Angeles in 1988, the Oilers kept winning. Edmonton won its final Stanley Cup in 1990.

STANLEY CUP WINS BY DYNASTIES

These five teams dominated the NHL for 55 years.

YEAR: 1946, 1950, 1960, 1970, 1980, 1990

- TORONTO MAPLE LEAFS
- DETROIT RED WINGS
- MONTREAL CANADIENS
- NEW YORK ISLANDERS
- EDMONTON OILERS

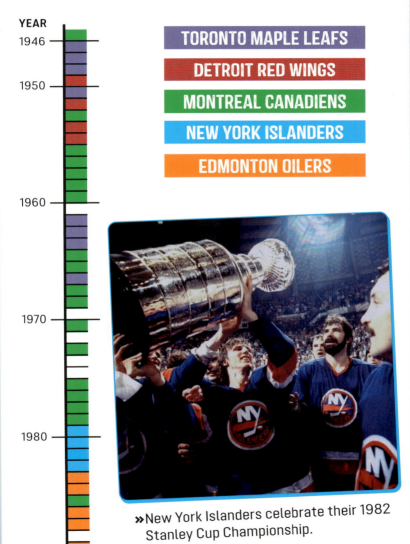

» New York Islanders celebrate their 1982 Stanley Cup Championship.

STANLEY CUP STANDOUTS

These teams have won the most championships:

Montreal Canadiens—24

Toronto Maple Leafs—13

Detroit Red Wings—11

Boston Bruins—6

Chicago Blackhawks—6

RECENT STANLEY CUP CHAMPIONS

2024	Florida Panthers
2023	Vegas Golden Knights
2022	Colorado Avalanche
2021	Tampa Bay Lightning
2020	Tampa Bay Lightning

A DAY WITH THE CUP

One unique aspect of the NHL is that each member of the championship team gets to have the Stanley Cup in their possession for the day. That has led to some interesting experiences.

END OF AN ERA

Team dynasties are harder to achieve these days. Free agency lets players go where the best contract offers are. That means players change teams more often than in the past. It strengthens some teams and can weaken championship teams.

The NHL draft also helps struggling teams by letting them pick some of the league's best young players. They can help lift a team back to success at the expense of a veteran squad.

Will there ever be another dynasty in the NHL?

Several teams have had solid windows of success since the Edmonton Oilers:

- The Detroit Red Wings have won back-to-back championships.

- The Pittsburgh Penguins have won back-to-backs twice.

- The Tampa Bay Lightning won the Stanley Cup in 2020 and 2021.

- The closest team to reaching dynasty status was the Chicago Blackhawks. They won three championships from 2010 to 2015.

Iconic Players

THE GREAT ONE

When it comes to hockey, Wayne Gretzky is the GOAT. In 1978, Gretzky joined the Indianapolis Racers in the World Hockey League (WHL) at just 17 years old. He was quickly traded to the Edmonton Oilers. When the WHL folded in 1979, the Oilers joined the NHL as an expansion team.

Using a dazzling mix of speed and skating ability, Gretzky made scoring look easy. He won four championships with the Edmonton Oilers before being sent to the Los Angeles Kings in a blockbuster trade. Many of today's players say that Gretzky inspired them to play the sport.

Gretzky was the NHL's leading career goal scorer for 31 years with 894. Gretzy is still the greatest assist producer with 1,963.

He earned the league's Most Valuable Player (MVP) award eight years in a row.

Gretzky scored more than 200 points in a year four times. He remains the only player in league history to reach that number.

YOUNG STARS
Today's top young players are among the best of the best.

SKATING: Tim Stützle
Center / Ottawa Senators
23.47 miles (37.77 km) per hour skate speed

SIZE: Owen Power
Defenseman / Buffalo Sabres
6 feet, 6 inches, 218 pounds

PASSING: Cale Makar
Defenseman / Colorado Avalanche
69 assists in a single season

GOAL SCORING: Connor Bedard
Center / Chicago Blackhawks
22 goals in his rookie season

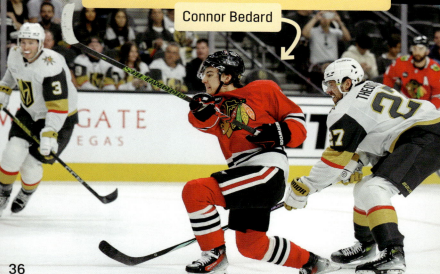
Connor Bedard

THE BROTHERS HUGHES

Jack, Luke, and Quinn Hughes made their December 2023 game a family affair. Jack and Luke play for the New Jersey Devils. Quinn starts for the Vancouver Canucks. They became the ninth trio of brothers to play in an NHL game.

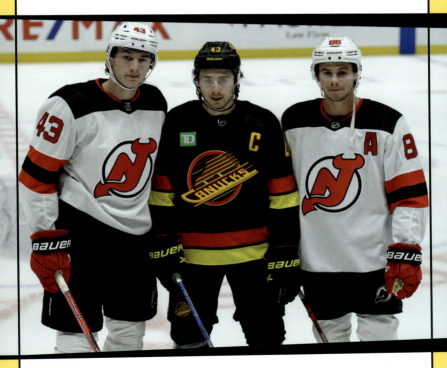

»From left to right: Brothers Luke, Quinn, and Jack Hughes pose for a photo after their December 2023 game.

BREAKING THE ICE

WILLIE O'REE was the first Black player in the NHL. He was called up from the minors to the Boston Bruins on January 18, 1958.

O'Ree finished his NHL career in 1961 after 45 games. He returned to the minors, where he played until 1979.

O'Ree's accomplishments have been honored by the sport and his native Canada. He was inducted into the Hockey Hall of Fame in 2018.

In 2022, on the 64th anniversary of his debut, the Bruins retired O'Ree's number 22 jersey in the Boston Garden rafters.

"From a young age, my heart and my mind were set on making it to the NHL. I'm grateful and honored that it was with the Bruins."
—Willie O'Ree

» Willie O'Ree's banner is carried on to the ice during his number retirement celebration.

Ovi's Office

As of April 2025, Alex Ovechkin had scored an NHL-record 324 power-play goals. Many came from the left face-off circle. This spot has earned the nickname "Ovi's Office" or the "Ovi Spot."

»Ovechkin (far right) shoots the puck and scores from his "office."

Ovechkin's teammates know exactly where to pass the puck to hit Ovi's stick.

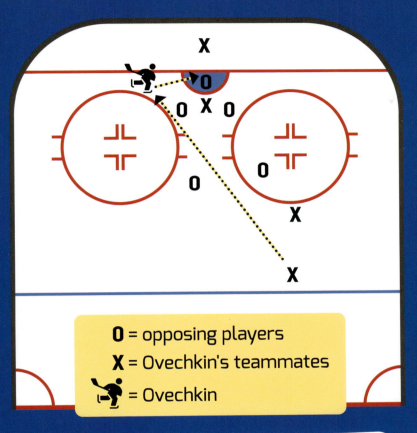

O = opposing players
X = Ovechkin's teammates
= Ovechkin

SURPASSING THE GREAT ONE'S RECORD?

Ovechkin scored his 895th goal on April 6, 2025, surpassing Gretzy's all-time scoring record in the same number of games—1,487. Guess where he made the shot from—his office!

Record Breakers

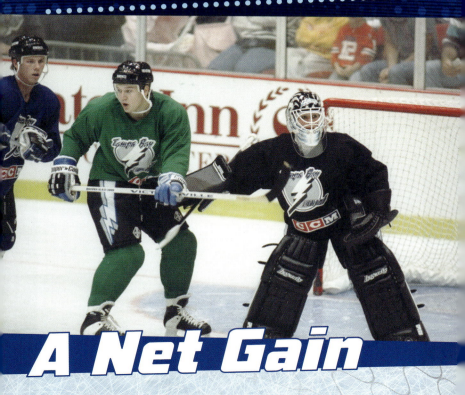

A Net Gain

Manon Rhéaume grew up playing hockey with her brothers in the 1980s. There were no women's hockey teams then. She became the first woman to play professionally in a major sports league.

In 1992, Rhéaume tried out as a goaltender for the Tampa Bay Lightning. Many people treated her tryout as a joke. But the Lightning announced she would play in a preseason game.

She played one period and allowed two goals. Rhéaume returned to Tampa Bay in 1993 and played in another preseason contest. While she didn't make the team, she did help open the door for increased women's participation in the sport.

Women's hockey became an Olympic sport in 1998. Rhéaume won a silver medal for Canada in the 1998 Olympics. She played professionally in men's and women's leagues until 2008.

WOMEN ON THE ICE

The Professional Women's Hockey League's first season was 2023–2024. It started with six teams. The Minnesota Frost won the championship over the Boston Fleet.

BEST OF THE BEST

Check out the NHL's all-time leaders in major categories.

	GOALS	895 (and counting)	Alex Ovechkin
	ASSISTS	1,963	Wayne Gretzky
	SHOTS ON GOAL	6,852 (and counting)	Alex Ovechkin
	HITS	4,029	Cal Clutterbuck
	SAVES	28,928	Martin Brodeur

Buzzer Beaters

There have been 491 goals scored with just one second remaining in the game. On December 22, 2023, the Rangers' Will Cuylle scored at the buzzer to give his team a 4–3 win over Edmonton.

» Will Cuylle shoots and scores in the final second of the game against the Edmonton Oilers on December 2023.

NHL's IRON MAN

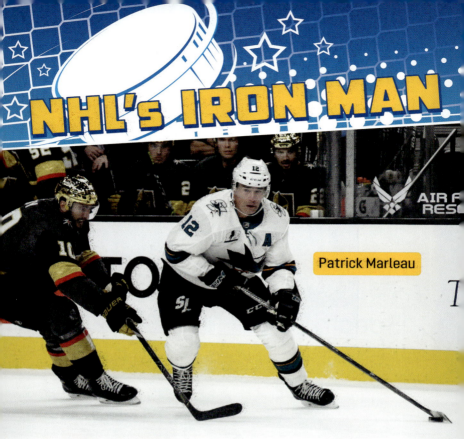

Patrick Marleau

Patrick Marleau set the record for all-time games played in the NHL regular season in 2021. He retired later that year having played in 1,779 games over 21 seasons.

Marleau played in 910 of those games in a row from 2009–2021. **Phil Kessel** has him beat in that category. He played in 1,064 consecutive games from 2009–2023.

Dan Ellis

SWEATING ON ICE

It takes a lot of energy to play hockey. Players often lose 5 to 8 pounds (2.3 to 3.6 kilograms) of sweat during a game. Goalie Dan Ellis, has even had to receive special fluids to recover!

About the Author

Elliott Smith is a freelance writer, editor and author. He has covered a wide variety of subjects, including sports, entertainment, and travel, for newspapers, magazines, and web sites. He lives in the Washington, D.C. area with his wife and two children.

More in This Series

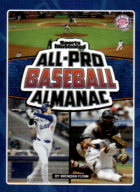
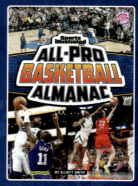
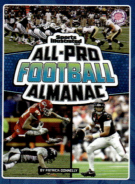
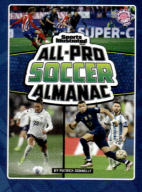